STAR WARS ADVENTURES

BOBA FETT AND THE SHIP OF FEAR

Script **Jeremy Barlow**

Art **Daxiong**

Lettering **Michael Heisler**

Cover **Sean McNally**

Dark Horse Books®

THIS STORY TAKES PLACE APPROXIMATELY TWO YEARS AFTER THE BATTLE OF YAVIN.

AN
AMBUSH...?

WHO...?

MAYBE NOT.

BUT I *DO* KNOW THAT I'M NOT SO DESPERATE...

...THAT I CAN'T TELL THIS *ARACHEDRON* SCULPTURE IS A FAKE.

KROOM!

12

YOU'RE KILLING US HERE! WHY NOT JUST SHOOT US WHILE YOU'RE AT IT?

BECAUSE THERE'S NO MONEY IN IT.

YOU'LL WISH YOU HAD. SOONER OR LATER, LEAVING US ALIVE IS GOING TO COST YOU.

IT'S GOING TO COST YOU *BIG.*

I'LL TAKE MY CHANCES.

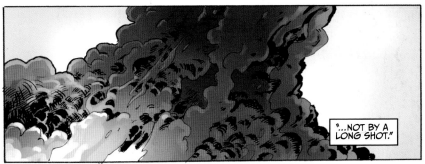

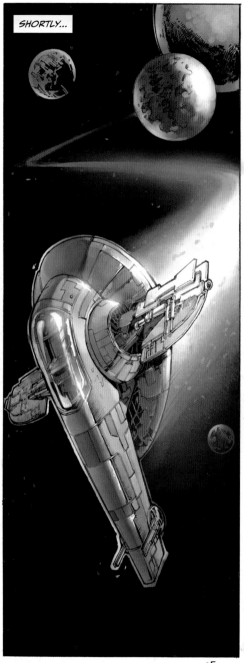

SHORTLY...

WHAT DO YOU HAVE FOR ME?

I FOUND IT -- BUT I FOUND SOMETHING ELSE EVEN BETTER...

"IN ITS DAY -- WE'RE TALKING *FOUR HUNDRED YEARS AGO* -- THE *REVERIE* WAS A TOP-OF-THE-LINE LUXURY CRUISER.

"RUMOR HAS IT *SIX PLANETS* WENT BROKE SPENDING TO BUILD IT.

"I DON'T KNOW ABOUT THAT -- BUT I *DO* KNOW THAT IT CATERED TO THE RICHEST PEOPLE IN THE GALAXY.

"JUST BUYING A TICKET COST MORE MONEY THAN *WE'LL* EVER SEE...

"...OR *I'LL* EVER SEE, ANYWAY.

"THING IS, FOR AS MUCH AS THEY SPENT ON MAKING HER LOOK PRETTY, THEY CUT CORNERS ON THE LITTLE THINGS --

"-- SMALL DETAILS LIKE FIRE CONTROLS AND SHIELDING SYSTEMS.

"A COUPLE YEARS INTO HER VOYAGE, SOMETHING BREACHED HER HULL AND -- ≷WHOOP!≷ -- DOWN SHE WENT."

I DIDN'T ASK FOR A HISTORY LESSON -- JUST TELL ME WHERE IT IS.

19

"AFTER THE ACCIDENT, SHE CHANGED HANDS A FEW TIMES. NO ONE COULD AFFORD THE UPKEEP, LET ALONE THE OVERHAUL SHE NEEDED TO FLY AGAIN...

"...SO THE OWNERS DID THE *RESPONSIBLE* AND *HONORABLE* THING...

"...THEY STRIPPED HER VALUABLES AND DUMPED HER AT A MASSIVE *SHIP GRAVEYARD* WAY OUT ON THE GALAXY'S EDGE.

"OUT OF SIGHT, OUT OF MIND, RIGHT?

"FOLKS HAVE BEEN DITCHING THEIR TRASH OUT THERE FOR CENTURIES, SO GOOD LUCK SPOTTING *THE REVERIE* IN THAT MESS...

"...IF YOU *DO* GET LUCKY AND FIND HER ON ONE OF THE JUNK FIELD'S OUTER EDGES, CHANCES ARE YOU WON'T BE ALONE...

HR-CHAK

HR-CHAK

SORT OF.
JUST THE CONCEPT
DESIGNS THEY
PITCHED TO THE
INVESTORS.

THEY
MIGHT BE MORE
WISHFUL THINKING
THAN ACTUAL
WORK PRINTS.

THAT'LL HAVE
TO DO. I NEED
YOU TO GUIDE
ME TOWARD THE
SHIP'S SECURITY
VAULTS.

NOT SURE IF THE POWER GENERATORS STILL WORK AFTER ALL THIS TIME, BUT IT'S WORTH A TRY.

PROBABLY BE A LOT EASIER FOR YOU TO MOVE AROUND WITH THE LIGHTS ON.

UH, ASSUMING THESE DIAGRAMS ARE ≳KSSH!≲ *CLOSE* TO ACCURATE, YOU ≳KSSH!≲ BE COMING UP ON THE ENGINEERING DECKS.

LOOK FOR A CONTROL CONSOLE WITH ≳KSSSHH!≲ OR A LEVER OF SOME KIND. THAT SHOULD FIRE UP THE GENERATORS.

FIND IT?

FOUND *SOMETHING.* BUT I'M LOSING *YOU* -- YOUR SIGNAL'S BREAKING UP. I'M CUTTING THE COMM.

≳KSSSH!≲ YOU SURE ABOUT THAT?

CHA-CHUNK!

25

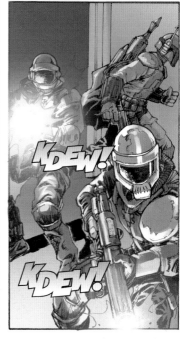

UHH...

THERE HE IS -- FINALLY. JUST *HOW HIGH* DID YOU CRANK YOUR STUN?

ARE YOU KIDDING? IT WAS ENOUGH TO DROP A WOOKIEE -- HE'S LUCKY HE'S STILL BREATHING.

I'M NOT TAKING ANY CHANCES WITH *HIM*.

KRAK!

COME ON, TOUGH GUY -- GET IT TOGETHER. YOU'VE KEPT US WAITING LONG ENOUGH.

"...AND *YOU'RE* AFTER THE *REAL* DEAL.

"ACCORDING TO LEGEND, THE ARACHEDRON WAS CENTRAL TO SOME ALIEN CULTURE THAT'S LONG SINCE DIED OUT.

"BUT AS THESE THINGS DO, THE SACRED RELICS BECAME VALUABLE TRINKETS FOR THE WEALTHY.

"IT'D PROBABLY STILL BE GATHERING DUST IN SOME MANSION RIGHT NOW...

"...IF IT WEREN'T CURSED."

IF YOU *BELIEVE* IN THAT JUNK, I MEAN. CAN'T SAY I DO, BUT YOU HAVE TO WONDER...

...IF IT HADN'T BEEN ABOARD *THE REVERIE* ON HER FINAL FLIGHT -- WOULD THE ACCIDENT HAVE HAPPENED?

IF THE ARACHEDRON EXISTS, IT'LL BE WORTH *MILLIONS.*

FOR ABOUT A HUNDRED YEARS OR SO AFTER THE ACCIDENT, FORTUNE HUNTERS FROM HERE TO *NAR SHADDAA* SET OUT TO PILLAGE HER HALLS...

...NONE CAME BACK ALIVE. WHICH MEANS YOU'RE NOT THE FIRST ONE WHO'S GOING TO DIE HERE, FETT.

BUT YOU *WILL* BE THE LAST.

THIS IS A BIG MOMENT FOR YOU AND YOUR BROTHER, EDO.

MAYBE YOU'LL FINALLY EARN THE *RESPECT* YOU'VE BEEN CHASING SO LONG.

MAYBE YOU WON'T LIVE SO DEEP IN YOUR FATHER'S SHADOW ANYMORE. THAT HAS TO FEEL GOOD.

YOUR DAD WAS ONE OF THE BEST THERE WAS -- I RESPECTED HIM. BECAUSE OF THAT, I WON'T SPOIL THIS FOR YOU. NOT YET, ANYWAY.

SO TAKE IT IN. ENJOY THIS MOMENT FOR ALL OF THE POTENTIAL IT PROMISES -- BECAUSE IT'S ALMOST PAST.

YOU'RE ABOUT TO REALIZE A HARD AND UNAVOIDABLE TRUTH...

YOU'RE RIGHT -- EVEN PUTTING THE MONEY ASIDE, WE STAND TO GAIN *A LOT* FROM THIS JOB.

I *KNOW* YOU, FETT. IF WE TURN YOU LOOSE LIKE YOU'RE ASKING, PRETTY SOON WE'LL BE FEELING YOUR *BLADE* IN OUR BACKS.

GIVE ME *ONE GOOD REASON* WHY I CAN TRUST THAT *WON'T* HAPPEN.

THERE ISN'T ONE. BUT I CAN'T GET THROUGH THIS SHIP'S INFESTATION ON MY OWN, EITHER -- I NEED YOU AS MUCH AS YOU NEED ME.

GOOD ENOUGH FOR ME.

EDO -- UNLOCK HIM.

WE TOOK YOUR JETPACK'S FUEL CELLS AND THREW YOUR RIFLE OVER THE SIDE.

TAKE THESE -- THEY'LL WORK IN A PINCH. THEY'RE KEYED TO OUR BIO-SIGNATURES, SO YOU CAN USE THEM, BUT YOU CAN'T USE THEM AGAINST *US.*

LET'S GET MOVING.

CLICK! CLICK!

HEY!

I HAD TO KNOW I COULD TRUST WHAT YOU SAY.

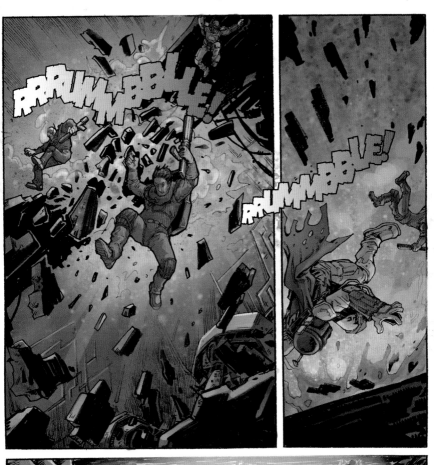

48

CALL IT WHAT YOU WANT-- JUST STOP BLAMING *ME* FOR YOUR SHORTCOMINGS.

YOUR OLD MAN WAS GOOD, NO DOUBT ABOUT IT...

...HE DID WHAT IT TOOK TO GET THE JOB DONE, AND SOMEHOW KEPT HIS HANDS CLEAN IN THE PROCESS.

BUT *YOU TWO*...

...YOU'RE DECENT BOUNTY HUNTERS -- YOU MIGHT EVEN BE GREAT SOMEDAY -- BUT NOT WHILE THE WEIGHT OF YOUR LEGACY DRAGS YOU DOWN.

AND IT'S YOUR OWN FAULT-- YOU EXPLOITED YOUR FAMILY NAME -- YOU PLAYED UP EXPECTATIONS THAT *NO ONE* COULD MEET.

NOW EVERY JOB YOU TAKE IS A FIGHT FOR LEGITIMACY AND RESPECT THAT YOU CAN'T SEEM TO WIN. I'D BE BITTER ABOUT IT, TOO.

IF YOU THINK KILLING *ME* AND WALKING OUT OF HERE WITH THE ARACHEDRON WILL CHANGE THAT, YOU'RE *WRONG.*

I'LL TAKE MY CHANCES.

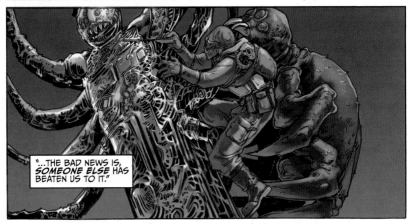

-- THAT'S A REAL NICE *SPIDER DISGUISE* YOU'RE WEARING...

...BUT HOW 'BOUT YOU JUMP ON DOWN HERE AND HAND THAT OVER?

ARE YOU *KIDDING* ME?

I'VE BEEN ON THIS SHIP FOR *TWO WEEKS* LOOKING FOR THIS THING -- YOU CAN'T JUST COME ALONG AND *SNATCH* IT AWAY FROM ME.

BELIEVE ME, I KNOW HOW YOU FEEL.

BUT THAT'S *EXACTLY* WHAT WE'RE DOING.

FRRRRRUMMMBLE!!

BOOM!!

I'D REALLY LIKE TO LEAVE NOW, IF THAT WORKS FOR EVERYONE.

IT'S NOT *US* THEY WANT. IT'S THIS ARTIFACT -- IT HAS SOME WEIRD HOLD OVER THEM.

WELL, THEY AREN'T GETTING IT. I HAVE *MORE* THAN ENOUGH AMMO TO GO AROUND.

THE ONLY WAY OUT IS THE WAY WE CAME IN -- WE HAVE TO CLEAR A PATH!

KDEW!

KDEW!

KDEW!

THAT'S NOT HAPPENING -- NOT UNLESS YOU WANT TO SWIM THROUGH THAT SEA OF SPIDERS TO GET THERE.

WE HAVE TO FIND ANOTHER WAY OUT, AND WE HAVE TO DO IT QUICK!

WHAT DID
YOU JUST
DO?!

HERE -- YOUR JETPACK'S FUEL CELLS ARE INSIDE.

YOU WERE RIGHT ALL ALONG.

DON'T BE CRAZY! YOU'RE NOT GOING AFTER HIM!

I HAVE TO. HE'S MY BROTHER...

...HE'S ALL I HAVE LEFT.

KKRR

UUMMBBLE!

I'VE HAD MORE THAN ENOUGH OF THIS PLACE. GOOD LUCK GETTING BACK TO YOUR SHIP.

I'LL PAY YOU *FIFTY THOUSAND* CREDITS TO GET ME OUT OF HERE!

CHA-CHIK!

I WAS THINKING A *HUNDRED* SOUNDED BETTER.

FINE! FINE -- OKAY!

STRAP YOURSELF IN -- THIS MIGHT GET ROUGH.

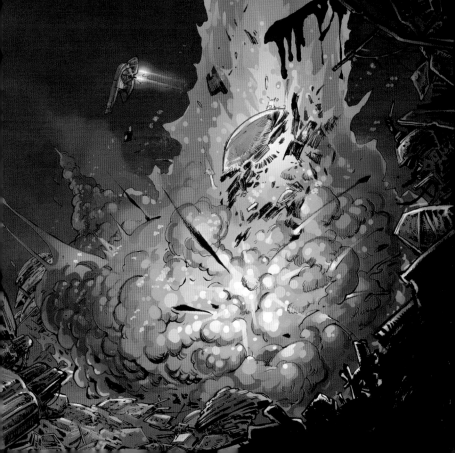

EVENTUALLY...

...*THERE.* THE FUNDS HAVE BEEN TRANSFERRED TO YOUR ACCOUNT -- ONE HUNDRED THOUSAND CREDITS. THAT ABOUT CLEANS ME OUT.

BUT I'D RATHER BE *BROKE* AND *ALIVE* THAN THE ALTERNATIVE.

IT SCARES ME A LITTLE, WHAT THOSE BROTHERS DID -- THROWING THEIR LIVES AWAY LIKE THAT.

I'VE SPENT A GOOD PART OF MY ADULT LIFE CHASING THAT ARACHEDRON. I MIGHT'VE CHASED IT INTO THE ABYSS RIGHT ALONG WITH THEM.

THAT MAKES ONE OF US. THE STROMS NEVER UNDERSTOOD THAT A BOUNTY HUNTER'S GREATEST ASSET ISN'T *CUNNING* -- IT'S SOUND JUDGMENT.

WHEN THE REWARD IS NO LONGER WORTH THE RISK, YOU CUT IT LOOSE.

IT'S AN UNFORGIVING LESSON...AND THEY LEARNED IT THE HARD WAY.

73

STAR WARS GRAPHIC NOVEL TIMELINE (IN YEARS)

Omnibus: Tales of the Jedi—5,000–3,986 BSW4

Knights of the Old Republic—3,964–3,963 BSW4

The Old Republic—3653,3678 BSW4

Jedi vs. Sith—1,000 BSW4

Omnibus: Rise of the Sith—33 BSW4

Episode I: The Phantom Menace—32 BSW4

Omnibus: Emissaries and Assassins—32 BSW4

Twilight—31 BSW4

Bounty Hunters—31 BSW4

Omnibus: Menace Revealed—31–22 BSW4

Darkness—30 BSW4

The Stark Hyperspace War—30 BSW4

Rite of Passage—28 BSW4

Honor and Duty—24 BSW4

Episode II: Attack of the Clones—22 BSW4

Clone Wars—22–19 BSW4

Clone Wars Adventures—22–19 BSW4

General Grievous—22–19 BSW4

Episode III: Revenge of the Sith—19 BSW4

Dark Times—19 BSW4

Omnibus: Droids—5.5 BSW4

Boba Fett: Enemy of the Empire—3 BSW4

Underworld—1 BSW4

Episode IV: A New Hope—SW4

Classic Star Wars—0–3 ASW4

A Long Time Ago . . . —0–4 ASW4

Empire—0 ASW4

Rebellion—0 ASW4

Boba Fett: Man with a Mission—0 ASW4

Omnibus: Early Victories—0–3 ASW4

Jabba the Hutt: The Art of the Deal—1 ASW4

Episode V: The Empire Strikes Back—3 ASW4

Omnibus: Shadows of the Empire—3.5–4.5 ASW4

Episode VI: Return of the Jedi—4 ASW4

Omnibus: X-Wing Rogue Squadron—4–5 ASW4

Heir to the Empire—9 ASW4

Dark Force Rising—9 ASW4

The Last Command—9 ASW4

Dark Empire—10 ASW4

Boba Fett: Death, Lies, and Treachery—10 ASW4

Crimson Empire—11 ASW4

Jedi Academy: Leviathan—12 ASW4

Union—19 ASW4

Chewbacca—25 ASW4

Invasion—25 ASW4

Legacy—130–137 ASW4

Old Republic Era
25,000 – 1000 years before
Star Wars: A New Hope

Rise of the Empire Era
1000 – 0 years before
Star Wars: A New Hope

Rebellion Era
0 – 5 years after
Star Wars: A New Hope

New Republic Era
5 – 25 years after
Star Wars: A New Hope

New Jedi Order Era
25+ years after
Star Wars: A New Hope

Legacy Era
130+ years after
Star Wars: A New Hope

Infinities
Does not apply to timeline

Sergio Aragonés Stomps Star Wars
Star Wars Tales
Star Wars Infinities
Tag and Bink
Star Wars Visionaries

BSW4 = before *Episode IV: A New Hope*. ASW4 = after *Episode IV: A New Hope*.

CLONE WARS ADVENTURES

Don't miss any of the action-packed adventures of your favorite STAR WARS® characters, available at comics shops and bookstores in a galaxy near you!

$6.99 each!

Volume 1
ISBN 978-1-59307-243-8

Volume 2
ISBN 978-1-59307-271-1

Volume 3
ISBN 978-1-59307-307-7

Volume 4
ISBN 978-1-59307-402-9

Volume 5
ISBN 978-1-59307-483-8

Volume 6
ISBN 978-1-59307-567-5

Volume 7
ISBN 978-1-59307-678-8

Volume 8
ISBN 978-1-59307-680-1

Volume 9
ISBN 978-1-59307-832-4

Volume 10
ISBN 978-1-59307-878-2